YOU DON'T KNOW ME

Orville Lloyd Douglas

TSAR Publications

We acknowledge the support of the Canada Council for the Arts
for our publishing program.
We also acknowledge support from
the Ontario Arts Council.

Cover design by David Drummond

Library and Archives Canada Cataloguing in Publication

Douglas, Orville Lloyd, 1976-
You don't know me / Orville Lloyd Douglas.

Poems.
ISBN 1-894770-22-6

1. Gay men--Poetry. 2. Blacks--Poetry. I. Title.

PS8607.O93Y69 2005 C811'.6 C2005-901569-1

Printed in Canada by Coach House Printing

TSAR Publications
P. O. Box 6996, Station A
Toronto, Ontario M5W 1X7
Canada

www.tsarbooks.com

Contents

I Am Not Black

What does black mean?
I am not black
This is the first thing you should know about me
When I look in the mirror certain people say I am not
   what I see in front of me everyday
I don't listen to rap music, wear hip hop clothes
I couldn't recall a Jay Z from a CD
I choose not to watch BET religiously as though
   some musician is Martin Luther King
Preaching the gospel while black youth empty their
   bank accounts paying for
A large mansion in a gated community which youth aspire for
To have women with large breasts who don't care about them
   say reassuring words
In their ear
I don't walk with a swagger, with my jeans down to my
   buttocks
I refuse to call the so called "fairer" sex
   a term analogous to a dog
I dream of becoming a great writer like Langston Hughes or
   James Baldwin
I write furiously, working hard for social change,
   for the world to be better
I can't wait around for Michael Jordan to be my father figure
I sucked at basketball in high school never ran track and field
   or played baseball
Last week I watched boxing for the first time only to become
   bored five minutes later
I see the boys at the local mall grown men wearing the same
   carbon copy clothes
They tell me they are thugs
I never aspired to be looked upon as a criminal
A menace to society I am not interested in impropriety

The gold jewelry, the polished $200 dollar Nike sneakers,
       the sweltering machismo
I don't slur my words together like an alcoholic
       on a drunken binge
I am gay , I love men and I live my life
Having the guts to be myself to love other men is my sin
I am now branded with the Scarlet Letter
Etched in my skin I have become a parasite the latest enemy
Yet I am not black I don't lie about my sex life
       nor do I have five babies out of wedlock
I don't have some woman calling me saying that I missed
       last month's child support
Nor do I have another guy chasing me down pleading
       that I pay up the drug money
Remember I am not black
I won't follow the collective mentality
That sing the sobbing song of woe is me I'm black
Take pity on me is the new hymn song
Reparations against slavery is not my main focus
Getting an education is the right prognosis
Nor is blaming the mainstream for all my problems in life
From failing third grade to not becoming a good violin player
Everyone is responsible for the shame that is my life
I can never ever be at fault or have any accountability
I am not black
I may be of African ancestry from my parents lineage
I have no intention of saying I know about mother Africa
The romanticized pleasure the dream of connecting to
       something
I forgot to buy the African traditional clothing and learn to
       speak Swahili
I am not black
My hair may be nappy at the roots
Skin as black as coal, knowledge of black history expanding

I've traveled across the antebellum era, through the Civil War
        back to Canada
Down the railroad I met Harriet Tubman, Mary Ann Shadd
        Cary, and Henry Bibb
Read Uncle Tom's Cabin and Huckleberry Finn
Sang the O Canada and believed in something
Love poetry, reading Zora Neale Hurston, and just
        being myself
You say I am not black
Well if I am not black
Then my friend
What are you?

Uppity Niggers

They say university is survival of the fittest
I've met the niggers all before
During my undergraduate days
Through the eyes of ambivalence
You've got you're know it all niggers.
You've got you're head niggers in charge!
You've got I'm better than you niggers!
You're the fucking hypocritical-niggers!
You're sell out niggers!
I had to censor myself while they preached in lectures
They talk the good fight though about our rights
You're wearing your Masters and Doctorate degrees
It's navy blue, gray, or brown three quarter length
It's tight, starched and well pressed for show and tell
Living behind the golden gates
Perched in the lighthouse that is their prosaic minds
In the glass towers is where they are
The press descend to the dinosaurs that preach down
To the so called unintelligent Nubian youth
After all the old know so much about us
Time to sell your new study that was too dumb
We are not like you
Yeah I'm talking to you nigger!
Your sermon you've memorized ten thousand times
Into the cracked mirror that is your chains
Now time for the *New York Times* best-sellers list
Flash that megawatt smile while you're on *CNN* or *NBC*
Patronize your sisters and brothers while peddling your
new three hundred page treatise
Is this your dissertation?
Does the money ever trickle back down to us?
Are you truly altruistic or just so oblivious
to your pretentiousness?

Tainted Windows

I know tainted windows
Yet the gray streaks of life clots the heart in Rexdale
Just like clockwork smokes of blood bleeds through the sky from
      dusk until dawn
Walls paper thin is no mystery to the misery of women who toil
      on Kipling Avenue
I recall the women in their nurse uniforms wiping the sweat
off their foreheads
Their varicose veins picking up groceries, children, toys, off
      the elevator floor
While their men disappear
As fire trucks extinguish one more midnight bonfire in
      the parking lot
At apt. 1510 I saw blackness smeared across the window pane
      of glass
I stood confused as a young boy glancing off my apartment
      balcony
As the lifeless form of a girl lay six feet under
Every morning another bag wrapped around a youth like a noose
The blood is unforgiving as it slivers on the cement
      it is a pool of melancholy
As fourteen-year-old girls with full wombs saunter by
      instead of hitting the books
While black men grab their big crotches slur their words
      with no swagger hunt the babies down
I understand the dust
I've seen the ashes
I know tainted windows

Welcome to Brampton

I experienced it a decade ago those propitious days
The elegant, white Victorian homes, charmed life,
        windswept streets
It was the dead giveaway of abundance
Polished teeth of suburbia, flashy black Porches
        and silver Lexus cars litter
The streets of Brampton
Chit chatting as their quiescent lives drift forward
Country golf clubs, fresh emerald manicured blades of grass
        is home
It reminds me of the plantations as they still drink Lemonade
        while we worked in hell
Slavery is the industrial warehouse
Made of steel, concrete, and wood
In another world spoiled milk, eviction notices, rats and
        roaches is pressure
Sex, falling backwards, welfare notices is this world's core
It's only five minutes away from utopia
Behind the golden gates of decadence
Are au pairs, and Asian nannies
While the boys in blue work overtime harassing our dark skins
As pregnant women in saris, men wearing turbans, and
        African gowns
Boil lifting heavy boxes to be delivered to the great white north
As the callous slave master cracks his whip of arrogance
A seventeen-year-old boy died behind these walls
Meal time cut short, lunch time nonexistent
The chains are invisible
As mom, dad, and the two kids uproot themselves
The "for sale sign" pitched on to the group
Mandeep, Jamal, Mariko will have to find new friends
Welcome to Brampton

Bottom of the River

I was born at the bottom of the river
North of the 49th parallel in a steaming pot of fire that is
      the city of Toronto
Tension boils across the melancholy, misty, murky waters,
      of Lake Ontario
Death is no sacrifice for truth
Beneath the cynical surface
Bubbling under is where black flesh rots
Black skin now dismembered as maggots crawl on corpses
Submerged below sewage, toxins, seaweed, mud,
      is where frustration breeds contempt
It spills on to the streets of Toronto as blood and bullets rain on
      all of us
Send them back to the Islands they say
I don't know the Islands
I never seen a palm tree, coconut, or the beautiful turquoise sea
      before
I don't know the terrain, the beaches, the sands of Jamaica
I never visited Kingston or Ocho Rios
I travelled from the bottom of the river across Canada
I heard the grumbles, whispers that float across on the subway,
      street car, or sidewalk
The brown, blue, green, and hazel eyes that glare with
      suspicion and contempt
Eyebrows scrunched, noses crinkling with disgust as the faces
      of Toronto reveal the truth
There must be something wrong I hear
But I'm not a killer
People have attempted to kill me with words, sentences,
      and false pretences
The murderers want to destroy my mind
As the men in blue pump cold steel into my black heart

My third grade teacher told me I couldn't read
After all I'm black she said
I was raised at the bottom of the river
Told that my thoughts, words, ideas, mean nothing
Stand straight black boy do as you're told said the third grade
　　　　school teacher
I was lectured that I can't speak I must learn the white man's
　　　　English
Patois is not a language I was told
Black history isn't Canada's history
Canada is Hockey Night in Canada, Molson beer,
　　　　and cold winters
I grew up at the bottom of the river
In a winter wonderland wasteland
A garbage dump where the dreams of the coloured men die
　　　　like a shooting in Rexdale
Demonized on the front page of print media is where
　　　　the corpses of black men toil
Dark skin, young mind, black just like me
I grovelled at jobs as a cashier, factory boy, garbage picker
I studied hard, never ran with the pack, went home before
　　　　nightfall
I turn on the news and I am branded as the enemy
This is supposed to be considered good employment they say
　　　　for people like me
Yet I rise I rise and I rise
I persist and I resist
I was preached at the bottom of the river about the façade of
　　　　multiculturalism
This ideal of a cultural mosaic is foreign to me since I am
　　　　considered an immigrant
The census calls me a visible minority
It's the politically correct term of being branded as "different"
　　　　or not the right colour
Yet it is not correct only fastidious

I never knew that I was visible
I always felt as though I was transparent as the air or a clean
sheet of paper
I was invisible
Yet I was born at the bottom of the river
My skin is not of the majority
Yet I am scorned to live the way of the white man
I was scolded to sing the O Canada in second grade
Yelled at by palefaced folks to praise the white
        Queen of England
I am told to be proud be a Canadian
What for?
What is a Canadian?
I don't know the Maple Leaf
I never camped in the woods or hunted in the wilderness
I'm not a farmer taking care of wheat, cows, and chicken in the
        plains of Alberta
I'm not from the Western prairies and I don't speak French
Nor do I eat pancakes and make homemade maple syrup
        every Sunday
I don't know Canada
I'm not white or a Quebecois
I will not die at the bottom of the river
North of the 49th parallel

The Knife

Life is like a knife
It slices the dreams of black boys
Like a slit wrist
Many of us won't make it to age thirty
A slashed throat
As some of us end in the clink
Lack of ambition bleeds
It's corrosive
Like hot fire
Burning
Scolding
Sizzling
It cannot
Be
Extinguished

When Dawn Breaks

When dawn breaks
I cry
As the red siren circles the neighborhood
This motion picture resumes day in and day out
No need for a new script, cast, or scenery
Another nigger bites the dust
Another drive-by as more dark corpses pile up
I flip through the daily news
Young, black, and male,
You look just like me
Except your eyes are dead
Lost baby you are lost

I tremble seeing your photo on the front page
I have the same black hands, black skin, brown eyes,
Am I a nigger just like you?
I scream
You fell into the trap
The oldest trick in the book
We grew up in similar neighbourhoods
Yet you are lying in a waste dump
As my tears drift down my face as it finds refuge
On my black heart
Every day when dawn breaks
The sharp edge of life
Keeps on ripping through
As dying dreams
Disappear
When dawn breaks
I slowly shift under the cotton sheets covering my face
Pulling out the radio
That the sharecroppers create
I will cover the sun with my bare hands
Causing an eclipse to occur
No blade of light to shine through
I won't let it in

Black Woman's Strength

I have seen you before
By my side helping me with algebra problems
Inside your luminous chestnut brown eyes
A fierce desire to succeed
To do better
I was born in hell yet you promised me we would leave
From Rexdale to Brampton we traveled from poverty to peace
When your forefathers were in chains
From the African continent to capitalist North America
You walk with the pitcher of the world on your shoulders
I see you now
In the supermarkets of Toronto lugging your groceries to
        the checkout counter
On the subway reading the financial section of the newspaper
At the parent-teacher night meetings demanding to know how
        your child is doing
Rubbing your daughter's shoulders encouraging her to read
        more
I know you deserve better
When will we all wake up?

In Search of James Baldwin

I found you under the dusty rustic books at the local library
        in Toronto
The bold black words on the pages speak volumes to you
I see myself in America right next to you in the year 1962
        and the red sirens
Surrounded us like vultures ripping apart prey
We were walking through Harlem at 10.00 pm when they
        threw bottles at us
You stood tall and firm as I trembled next to you
The boys in blue watched and laughed since this is their duty
We dare to live this is our crime
I am not frightened since you are still here
Your stories burn with fierce pain and anger yet resonate in my
        mind
I learned about the shadows that still remain
        of burning crosses and black bodies
Black bodies that have been shot, mutilated, lynched,
        and hung to dry in the wind
It is not 1962 but you reminded me time is linear it doesn't
        stand still

Freedom Reigns

Freedom surges through my veins
You rushed and got over three hundred slaves across the
        Canadian border
When you felt down and out of spirit your strength carried us
        on
We glide off your emotional flow gathering energy
We pray that tomorrow will be better than today
Your brown eyes are luminous and are an Oasis of calm in this
        thunderstorm of terror
Inside the cellar we wait for days sometimes weeks hoping no
        one will find us
Porridge, cornmeal is our staple our saviour
The henchmen are galloping on their horses have an arrest
        warrant for you
They say you are a fugitive and that they want you
        dead or alive
From the depths of the south through swamps
        to the deciduous north you move
Over rolling plains and deep valleys across mountains
        they search for you
Remember Philadelphia when master saw you by the Liberty
        Bell
Throwing the chickens into the air saved us from the menacing
        pain
You say you can still feel the welts on your back
No more picking cotton in the blistering sun and pricking our
        fingers
No more spreading our legs
Freedom is not far away
When you are with us
This is freedom

Worse

There is nothing worse in this world than to be black and gay
It's a maximum security prison sentence of unhappiness and
        shame it is a century of pain
It's the chains that shackle the phrenology of the spirit
It stigmatizes, ostracizes, denigrates you
It is just a sharp shade of gray
Never ever is there any parole
It's a first degree lifetime of resentment that quietly atrophies
        the soul
It's like mourning at a wake for somebody you didn't care for
It's the twisted dying dream of pretending to be someone
        you're not
Hanging on to a rope strangles the last strand of hope you had
There is nothing worse in this world than to be voiceless
Since silence equals quiescence and imprudence
Unrequited betrayal comes to fruition
It's the boredom of disgrace
As being discarded into the waste of distilled nightmares
There is nothing worse in this world than dissemblance
Looking at people who look like you yet their eyes translate
Hypocrisy and contempt
You know that words are homicides that are worse than a car
        crash
Twisted sentences, smashed paragraphs, and burnt stanzas
        destroy
It's like waiting for a train wreck
Seeking a gun shot
Standing still as the crackle of lightning strikes you down
There is nothing worse in this world than reticence

Unspoken Truths

I escaped with a university degree
Battled my way through educational colonialism and
        Eurocentric philosophy
My mouth was taped shut for four years
Yet the lie is free speech is for anyone
Clearly not if you're black like me
I walked with the weight of the world on my back
As the coarse rope of white supremacy was tied across my
        burning wrists
University claimed they taught me about my "rights"
I never had any rights at university
University had all the rights
It's just for the whites
They got the largest student group office on campus
While the black student office is the size of a cardboard box
Can't use a megaphone at university
You'll be expelled for three years
You will be constricted like you were guillotined if you don't
agree   with their view
A white female official bluntly said: "We're not some small
        African nation that can't run their own elections."
The Queen on top didn't smash down her iron fist
        though on that statement
She just swept it under the rug
Just like all other race issues at university
In 1992 a theatrical production that was anti-black was
        splashed across Toronto
Of course this play was praised
The Mayor of Toronto claimed he was afraid of Africa
After all he said he would have been thrown into a pot and
        skinned alive
The media was silent in university about that though
Because remember black rights don't matter

I learned at university if you're black you've got to step back
Although they speak platitudes about diversity
It's all about "diversity" they say
When only sixteen out of over 1308 profs are black we all know
        what "diversity" means
When only one black is on the hiring committee
Sit back blacks don't talk back
Diversity means the majority of the black studies courses are
        taught by whites
When less then ten professors are black women
I know I know
You've heard this broken record before
The white black studies prof got mad when I asked about his
        "authenticity" about blacks
I didn't know that a white was the authority over black
        history?
He claimed he was a minority too
Now I know being white means you can claim you're a
        minority
I forgot the golden rule that whites run university
Remember the forty-percent grade I got on an essay
        after I wrote about the lack of "diversity"
Next, university claimed I was "out of line"
In 1992 when our older brothers and sisters packed the
        president's office
When angry white security officers asked for identification
        from all black students
The hazel, green, brown and blue eyes were laced with venom
        at the blacks
Don't forget when you walk through hell
You are not you anymore you've got to conform
I thought university was about speaking your mind
Not at all!

Mein Kampf

Whenever I look above at the Maple Leaf beneath the surface
        is a blazing Swastika
Below the fibers, fabric, threads of Canada is a raging disease
        called ambivalence.
Eyes are the illusions as the sharp black tentacles devour the
        spirit
I've been told to feel it, smell it, taste it, this fungus called
        freedom
This freedom isn't tangible though it is a death sentence
The Reichstag has created this new disease called diversity
This epidemic is dispersed across the satellite dishes, radio
        waves, digital channels
Diversity is malleable it's a raw virus that alters the mind,
        body, and soul

Der Führer demands that all buy into this rhetoric of the
        broadcasters who send their
Propaganda this resembles the Aryan nation
I sit on the black sofa transfixed by the blonde blue-eyed
        Fräulein and Herr
I don't look like them
Yet equality kills, it strikes out and slashes the flesh of the
        proletariat
Diversity is Mein Kampf

Quickly the Third Reich claims there is less Lebensraum for
        outsiders
Guess that means strippers from Eastern Europe get a free pass
        while hard working
construction workers from Latin America worry about the SS
        and the Gestapo
Liberty here means schwarz have no rights
Forty-seven percent of schwarz women live in poverty

Storm troopers shoot and kill schwarz there is no justice no
    dignity
Yet I am told to be good and say guten Tag and guten
    Morgen.

Stereotype

Close your eyes and you will see me
Hear my voice now you are deaf
Feel my pain the skin is numb
Open your mind now it is blank
Tell me am I real?

Big Black Cock

In a twisted turn of events I listened to you
Partly out of sheer boredom and nostalgia
A vortex of sexuality swirled around me as I played your game
It was puzzling at first since I was catching up to the scheme
        and dirty language
I could have been finished reading a volume of poetry as you
        attempted to be seductive
Throbbing hypnotic dance music in the background
You spoke in a serious tone and asked if I had a big black cock
I wanted to forgive you since it was 3:30 am and you could
        have been drunk
Can't you treat me like a man?
Ignorance overrides decent sensibility
Your voice rose as you let out a sigh
Don't touch me!
Motherfucker!
Is that all I am to you?
Am I just a long oak tree for your jungle fever aspirations?
You specifically asked if I had a big black cock that was dark
as   steel and big like a fire hose
Next you inquired if I love to fuck ass!
Colonize somebody else with your imperialistic ideals
Don't try to carve me up as the criminals did to Africa
I'm not some chocolate boy for your perverted fantasies
I have sliced through your shitty gibberish
Some dark-skinned folk will gladly bend over for a
        pale-skinned fool
But you don't want to know what is in my mind
Or what is in my soul

Nice Boys

She in a satin gown he is in a tuxedo
They are in their element of glory
Walking in to the lily-, tulip-, gardenia-covered gazebo
Roses, daisies, chrysanthemums are on display
Two hundred and fifty guests are ready to serenade you
The glowing chocolate cake rests on the immaculate marble
       table
In the lush garden is where dreams collide with fantasy
As a canopy of deciduous trees casts a shade across the field
The pastor's broad grin
While he flips through pages of the holy text
Resonates in my mind
While I stand in the background
Faded like a photograph
Where cynicism lives
Trapped in the archives of deceit
I thought I was a nice boy
University educated
Gregarious personality
I thought I was a nice boy
I once believed I could get married
No one would attend though

I can imagine the day
Two tuxedos two smiles two black hands
The kiss
The well wishers
Not today
I am not the
Black nice boy

Directions

Directions have eluded me
They haunt me as pain still lingers like a tick
That has engorged through piercing my spirit
It's red as a bouquet of fresh red roses
An omen that continues to be elusive
As time transpires

Directions are bruises I refused to follow
Sores that turn black and blue
Seconds only derailed the last decision
The jagged edge next to the skin, the circular white pill,
        the Vodka
Faith floats through fingers like a rain of crimson pouring out
        of flesh
Dreams of someday being a somebody
A detour of discarded dreams on the road to hell
Could it be that I deserve this?

Muted Party

Sweltering heat couldn't stop the Calypso music pulsating
               from the moving trucks
Lakeshore Avenue sizzled with glittery bold costumes
          in white, gold, blue, on display
Women with pugnacious breasts danced seductively to the
         Reggae beat
Men salivating on their ice cream cones stared in the distance
The party is muted as the men in blue stand in front of
         barricades
Walkie-talkies transmit coded messages
Some stupid nigger had to pull the trigger
The party is over
The past plays strange tricks on everyone
 Life ends when terror wins
This is the iron fist of City Hall at work

Painless

It
Will
All
Be
Painless
You
Said
My
Boyish
laugh
Answering
The
Telephone
Reassurances
Were
Presented
As
I
Stumbled
Towards
You
Into
A
World
Of
Melancholy
At
3:00 am
In the morning
Like
A
criminal
You

Lurked
By
The gas station
Pretending
To
Pump
Fuel
Into
Your black Porsche
I Stood
Yet
Sauntering
In
The
Direction
Of
Despair
Entering
Your
Vehicle
You grumbled
The moment would be
Painless
You
Promised
Me
I
Bent
Over
As
You
Stuffed
Your
Manhood
Inside

Panting
Like
A
Dog
Pounding
Your
Way
Through
Me
It
Is
All
Painless
You
Said
As
You
Bludgeoned my innocence
Bleeding
Pleading
You
Deceiving
Me

Fifteen minutes later
Like a slave I am
Tossed from your vehicle
On to the road
Where confusion
Exists
Within
Me
Painless
You
Say

Did
You
Not
Know
I
Was
Only
Seventeen

Tenderly

This kiss is for your wife
My tongue runs down on your spine like I did yesterday
And the day before
This broken record commences at midnight
At the same seedy motel
We lay on lascivious sheets
A brown patchy colour
I clenched the cold hard cash
While you sobbed about missing
Your five-year-old son's hockey game last week
I grab your hand
While your fifty-five year-old greased skin touched mine
I held your obese body
Tenderly
Smothering the last ounce of energy
Into you
Until sixty minutes is up

The Streets Are Your New Daddy

Now I know where you went
Into the direction of the elixir that numbs your anger
No compass was necessary to find you
The proof of your ingenuity was all over your solemn face
Pleasure is hearing a grown man grunt and groan for an
       orgasm
You, white and male middle-aged with cash to spend
The streets are your new daddy
Daddy will protect you from the knife of truth that slices at
       your soul
Daddy do you want to get spanked again?
Daddy your mouth is swollen from all of the ground level
       work
Did daddy cum faster this time?
You are just like all of the suburban daddies that drive down
       town late at night
Your wife knows the drill she doesn't want to go down on you
So might as well make somebody else's son do the job
Tender words sliver through cynical ears
Broken bottles, hotel suites, feces, rat poison, and raunchy
       sex is your occupation
It's a tough job to lose yourself every night
Into the arms of a man who hates you
His smooth warm blue eyes may say otherwise yet his motives
       reveal disgust
Underneath his cool demeanor a man is just a man
Who when probed will unleash his menacing fury
Striking you with his bloody, jagged, torn, brutally honest
       words and confessions
He clings to a life less than ordinary in the north
He prays that his life is different
But you know he can't
Life is like a painting in detail he has a fairytale ending

Except you're not in it
You've been brushed out
Like you parents did to you last summer
His semen laced with spit slides down your naughty throat like
    acid
As you struggle to drink his corrosive fluid
While his conscience coats your face the colour white
This is your duty
You relish the role of vixen
Why didn't you give a damn about you?
The pricking doesn't stop as hopelessness trickles through your
    veins
It now controls you
You combed through the dirty seedy, sex-driven streets of Toronto
Close to Yonge street where sin and excess combined into a
    grenade of deceit
Crack whores, prostitutes, and homeless folk down on their luck
    hit the pavement
You're bastard
What happened to that degree you were studying for?
Life wasn't supposed to end up like this when the nights sky is
    twinkling with stars
You always were such a dreamer
Lost boys such as yourself end up here
Daddy didn't bring any candy this time
Just like the other boys you see all the daddies driving up to the
    curb
The flashy Porches, Jeeps, Mazdas, Renaults, at midnight race
    towards you
Standing by the edge of this world you wait patiently like a young
    child
Wondering, pondering, thinking, that tonight's daddy will be
    sweet
You feign your age
There is no lost innocence tonight

In this sea of discontent you were swept into the vehicle of
       despair
Travelling down Yonge street to an alley with your new daddy
Hopefully daddy won't be angry this time   ·

Lady of the Night

Dear Cassandra
You are eternally asleep
Sweet princess your spirit still shines
It glistens, it glows within all of us
Yet your silhouette leaves an imprint on my mind
You were a survivor Cassandra
My dear trying to achieve the best you knew how
You succeeded you are a somebody Cassandra
A lady of the night

Lurking in the shadows are the married men you
met when night fell
Cassandra you gave these men the gift of love
Although some will call you a freak of nature
You gave them pleasure and hope
After the tragedy silence speaks volumes
It strikes a chord it proves the system
Doesn't work since you were the wrong colour
You would have been on the cover of every magazine
Cassandra we love you

I Know

I know you
I know your sagging dilapidated breasts
The stringy black hair you dye to turn back the clock to 1982
I know your house from the French windows to the golden
      faucets of your bath tub
No foundation or makeup will ever save you
I know the lines that are a continent of skin across your
      decrepit face
Folds of flesh that are valleys of unhappiness you desperately
      attempt to forget
Mountains of Botox treatments can't cure your reality
I know the crow's feet that are splinters of bitterness that
reveal the road of lies you keep
The threads of depression, of suicide attempts, of rage
      intertwine with your personality
I know the emptiness of your cold brown eyes is your detour
I know the soft touch that bring your mate to an orgasm
I know the shallowness of your life
Drowning in excess mixed with Vodka
The tea parties, antique furniture, golden jewels and diamonds
      are your drugs
You are addicted to the allure of materials not love
I know your favorite restaurants, galleries, opera houses
Your spirit is opaque lacking clarity
I know behind the lonely ocean of tears behind your sparking
      façade
Beneath the forty-thousand dollar gowns
I know you are in agony
The turbulent currents of guilt you use as a weapon
To keep your spouse your prisoner
I know the tired nights when your insomnia causes doubt of
      his absence

I know your wedding, birthday showers, and anniversary
    photos
I know the argument that you had last Thursday
We kiss the same liver spots on your spouse's spine
Yet you don't know me
I do know you
Every Sunday night he visits me
At the same place
Complaining about you to me
My back against the salacious sheets with him on top panting with
    sweat
I feel the brute force of a man
I know the testosterone strength crushing my spirit
I know the insatiable hunger of a man
I know the ferocious explosion of passion between his loins
His tongue slides across my cheeks, my cock, my ass, my chest,
    and my legs
His lips intertwine with mine while I gag
It will only be one hour
He clenches our hands together to cement our destiny
His kisses drenched with pain as he forces his mouth against me
After a few sips of Moet he sighs
The sentences tinged with regret escape his solemn lips
Dreaming of being somewhere else except here

Good Friend

My good friend
Gave me
Sweet candy and Doritos potato chips
Swiftly you drove me to your condo
Your forty-five-year old body crushed my bones
I am gorgeous you say
I stare at the white stucco ceiling
I am beautiful you reply
As your decrepit tongue licks my ebony skin
Wishing I could die in my sleep
I am everything you tell me
Come on come on
You plead
The boys in Cuba didn't mind
Photographs you splashed across the bed
Fourteen- and fifteen-year-old youths
Smiling for a pair of jeans
My legs are stretched apart
I am special so special you say
While I scream in agony
As you pray to survive
Just for one more day
I don't want to end up like them
My good friend
Tell me you love me

No

I am still waiting for you to stop penetrating me
You fisting my black ass while I grovel over a leather sofa
Crouched in the doggy style position in your office
Your fingers and tongue do all the dirty work
If only your pupils can see you now
Begging me to ejaculate into your mouth
I'm waiting for the pain to decrease from my rectum
If only your wife that makes sweet cupcakes and apple pie
       who saw you
Yet my anus is burning it scorches like an explosion
My algebra and geometry textbooks fall out of my knapsack
I said no
You pull my torn jeans down to my ankles
Placing your hands on my privates
Your saliva rolls over me
I scream no
Rubbing your fists against my buttocks
I yelled no
You slap me telling me to be a good black boy
When will you ever stop?

You Don't Know Me

You don't know me
My black skin
My thoughts
My ideals
Are transparent to your raging hormones
You don't see me
Even though we live in the same neighborhood
I sat next to your son in my Algebra class
I'm the whore that makes you happy
After you finished a new market merger
You fling your pressed cotton shirt on the bed
Seducing me with lies
I am pestered to pucker up
Plant a kiss delicately on to your decrepit lips
Tasting the venom that is destruction
I sucked your cock
I realized
You don't care
After all you had a business meeting
I rolled down your navy trousers
Kissing your firm erection
The semen coated my mouth
As you laughed
You don't know me
The next time
Will be the same

Unhappiness Now

Six years passed and still no document of your success
Seventy two months yet no photograph, lush ceremony
        or gown
Three hundred and twelve weeks have flown by and you are
        still stagnant
Where is the proof they ask one last time?
Your family now ignores you at the dinner table
You were the feast instead of the thanksgiving turkey
They carved at the little self-confidence you had and snapped
        into two like a bone
Their wish hasn't come true yet
Remember unhappiness is right now
Sadness doesn't die as you gloat in the sewer of self loathing
You were encouraged by pill popping psychiatrists to enjoy
the   filth that is your life
The diagnosis was you have some bizarre form of disorder
        drugs can cover
It must be bipolar or manic depression
Your sanity has been shipwrecked five years ago smashed
        against the coast of your
Deceptive nightmares
Xanax, Zoloft, Paxil, and Prozac can't cure your agony
It's easy to slay the dragons that keep on destroying you
Some keep on telling you the pain inside of you is invisible like
        a lynching in Alabama
In the year 1922
Strung up to die the asphyxiation process will only take a few
        minutes
Uncertainly imploded your mind
Suffering is too easy a word to describe you
Lectures, discussions, tutorials, together with café latte can't
        solve the riddle
Death is desolate and distinct like a California beach vacant on

a Sunday morning
Unhappiness is now as you persist to grovel in this ineptitude

My Name Is Orville

He's been dead the past 28 years
Buried under a quarry of shame
The loser, the hypocrite, the sodomite
Through the lens of purgatory
I see the essence of him
Lurking, shifting, sulking
It's visceral
Got that strange sounding name
After the popcorn maker
His leaden eyes are the weight of ecstasy

His broken record is a derelict of complacency
Made the bad choice not to attend arts school
Should have been on broadway
Once had that pearly white smile
It could have taken your breath away
Where is his Tony award?
Why hasn't he dined at the Russian Tea Room?

Loved Mozart, Dvořák, Wagner

Dropped out of university
Graduated an eternity later
He's shackled to this "degree"
The marionette of debt holds him prisoner
A BA doesn't mean you're free

Falling off the calendar
He's the freak you pelted with rocks
The faggot you snicker at behind his back
The unemployed black man
A guy you taunt on the subway platform
Looking at the rusty tracks
Wandering
Moving towards the Bloor viaduct
Looking down
wondering, wondering, wondering

The White Light

When the white light shines so brightly
Don't feel sorrow or regret my dear
Dive, Dive, Dive
Into the uncharted Ocean of unspoken despair
Submerge yourself seeking clarity and reason
Search, Search, Search
Through the murky waters of capricious currents
When you arise think of reality
Feel, Feel, Feel,
When the last gasp of breath engulfs you
As the eyelids flutter
Slowly, Slowly, Slowly
Watch, Watch, Watch,
When the eternal sleep begins
Remember the truth

Uncompromising Pain

Like a butcher's machete I keep on taking the thrashing to
        the skull
Beating down on me time and time again is the yearning for
        you to stop
But of course you don't
It's too easy to see me clinging to you like a sadistic man
        in a cult
I have been pitched your sermon and you hauled me into your
        lair
Cut into two pieces I'm ready for the slaughterhouse
You slash me into two yet no blood seeps through my veins
The words you speak are torture
I'm ready for the burning to commence
For the crowd to start chanting, screaming, yelling,
As the undertaker grabs the coarse noose to pull me back to
        reality
The torches are ready, the flame is a bright red as the oil
        slithers down
I stand before the mob pleading my case as the undertaker
        places
The death sentence around my throat as I gag for breath
While my flesh becomes constricted in agony thinking of you
Your harsh judgment prickled my flesh as it became engorged
Into a purplish colour filled with your venom
There is another side to every story
Yet everyone casually forgets me
As time strangles the truth
It twists, swirls, mutates into another meaning
It pulls, pushes, forces, that are distortions
The swearing, the derogatory language, the everything that I
        didn't want to believe
About you
Yes this is uncompromising pain!

African American Knight

It's not the tall, dark, muscular Olympic athlete that I seek
Nor the macho, arrogant executive from Los Angeles or
       Chicago
While taking a promenade in Central Park as the golden,
       emerald,
Amber blades of grass cascade on the field I think of you
A torrential downpour plunged on us as you held me under
       your
Magnificent black umbrella shielding me as you guided my
       steps
the puddles of my impatience

Sitting on an oak bench as the pain of the precipitation
       subsides
He kisses me oh so gently, or so lovingly oh so tenderly.
He's got the suave graciousness of Hughes, the intellect of
         Baldwin
and the brutal honesty of Wright
He held my hand undeterred as we cemented our destiny as
       we crossed the
Bronze brownstones in Harlem into the halo halls of the
Apollo
Placing the ring on my finger in a crowd of Nubian faces was
         bold as they gawked

Oh African American Knight show me the language of the soul
Teach me to decipher the courage of the heart and spirit
Love me like an African warrior
Protect me from me

As I drift from slumber into consciousness
I return to the static darkness of Toronto
A blizzard of cowardice and madness

No brothers hold hands here on Yonge street or Bayview
    avenue
No archives of our existence in this universe north of the 49th
    Parallel
Oh African American Knight take me with you
Across the Hudson River through to the shores of
Liberty, Freedom, and Opportunity
Away from this stagnant turbulent reality

Always

I will always remember when darkness shines on the horizon
and love to stare at that shining blue moonlight
I will always cherish the thread of life that floats
through the veins of leaves that are tragically
changing colour from a sunflower tinged yellow,
to a dark orange, and a bloody crimson red

I will always love the snow that is the colour of an oyster shell
I will always believe that everything shifts since
time is linear it doesn't stand still

The Awakening

I feel it, I sense it, I suck it, I want it,
During my slumber your manhood rises
It tickles, it moistens, it awakens me
I turn my body to see your ebony face next to mine
When your luscious touch reaches me an internal force takes
        over
I'm drowning in an oasis of pleasure
Never let me go
Hold me
Love me
As our bodies drip in drenched sweat
By the windows we lay wrapped in silk sheets
My legs shiver as your hands touch mine
It's almost as though I am somnambulistic hoping this is real
Prick me my beloved so I won't be inconsolable
Dreams are energies
As your strong, manly, beautiful arms touch me
No more pain, regret, and pain
Just this ambition that we can go anywhere together
I wrapped my heart around you
Please don't leave
I hope life can always be
Like this

The Final Hour

Beyond the phoenix coloured skyline
Behind the flickering energy of our lust
Beneath the last breath of our passion
Below the cumulus clouds I think of you
Because as the smoldering gust of wind moved I was
wondering, hoping, thinking, pondering of us
Between us we are burning burning like the Sahara
But the gulf is as wide as the Atlantic Ocean
Belligerent as you always are
Being bold cloaks the truth that has transpired
Beloved our final hour has passed

When I See Him

I wish one day that when I see him
Again that he will believe in me
He will look at me again
That he will never forget that passion
Exists between our lips
When our tongues touch love
Is all that we have
When I see him I want him to stare
Into my warm gregarious brown eyes
Discovering that love is something eternal
Not ephemeral it can survive
In the corridors of Vari Hall
He glances at me and I can tell
That we were meant to be together
Despite the trauma that he dwells in
When I see him
He provides me with so much self-confidence
He believes in me to be me
Our love is almost suicidal it is preventing us
From seeing the truth

I Owe You Nothing in Return

We are standing here in darkness in a subversive world
I look into your capricious languid brown eyes
Seeing nothing except a slaughterhouse of deceit
I have trampled across this wilderness ground before
Crossed the gravel path of imaginary dreams
Of being something to you
We collided together several times incognito
Questions emerged of your history to the map of the door
        of no return
Yet there is a wall of dissemblance
I wanted to decipher you
I owe you nothing in return

My Eyes

See the black sky
The desolate blue moon
The bleak heart
My eyes are oracles they know the turbulent unwavering
      ocean
The rippling current that turns a sweet tide into a
      thunderstorm
This feeling
Within my eyes
That sees
The continent of skin that is yours
Legs twisted like vines
Together
This is my destiny
Jagged, ripped, torn is me
Drowning deeper
Deeper into your subconscious
Seeing with my eyes
That are brown trembling
And knowing
You

April at 2:00 pm

We agreed to meet in April at 2:00 pm
I starched and pressed a matching brown shirt with matching
        khaki pants
Optimistically I dreamed of a Nubian King just like in a James
        Baldwin novel
Like Rufus I too was lost in New York City now I am in
        another country
I walked into the coffee shop in the queer world
Saw the freaky fags in hot pink gossip about their vacant lives
Waiting for you was like a century of absence
The cold blank stares bore me as I drank my herbal tea
Brimming was my confidence until I saw you
Right into your hollow, obligatory, soulless, brown eyes
I shook your dry black hand
You feigned your accent trying to sound like a white man from
        Rosedale
Do you remember Jamaica?
When our forefathers scrapped their way to peace
In the dimly lit restaurant the piercing silence was defeating

The man I speak to now is an imposter
Your white mask haunts you
Dark turbulent waves of the Rhine river swept you under
As you went on and on about Deutschland
You're still trapped like the Berlin Wall
Where is the real you?
You tell me I am ugly
Yes I have a broad nose, thick chocolate lips, kinky curly hair
The façade you live suits you

Divergent Paths

You say I am stubborn as a newborn child
Disrespectful, truculent, so immature that I hold on to you
Unwilling to adapt to new situations
This city is just not for me
You are mellifluous!
Towering buildings block a blade of civilization to shine
        through
This is claustrophobic hell
Molding walls too paper-thin
It's a one room sewer of contaminated syringes, broken bottles,
dirty floors with rodents
Wedged between death and suicide is no compromise
Pain has always been your predilection!
The silhouettes in the hallway demonstrate that crack is for
        everyone including you
Violence tears across the walls as high-pitched screams bounce
as a soundboard
The garbage-ridden streets and increased pollution traps the
        sky
The litmus test has proven correct
More traffic, arrogant taxi drivers, bellowing people cause
        irritation
The view of the lake is an environmental disaster
        of a grotesque, ghoulish, green, colour
You say my flaws ripple as a current of water
Inconsistent, precarious, aloof, are the strikes you shoot at me
You reload your ammunition targeting my essence saying I am
        intangible
How is that so?
I am real as blood that boils through my veins
My ideals are not transparent as the air you breathe
We are on divergent paths
Parallel yet never touching physically or emotionally
Away from this predicament is my sanctuary

Alone

Alone
Am
I
On
The
Sidewalk
Grovelling
Like
A
Lunatic
The
Scent
Of
Whiskey
And
Gin
Engulfs
Me
Ecstasy
Was
For
Good
Measure
Numbs
The
Mind
Eyes dilated
Spinning around
Like a hobo
Calling out
To
Someone
Anyone
Yet
No
One
Hears

Stacked Books

We speak in hushed tones over the green tea at the café
Sipping the green tea that is the colour of our destiny
Stirring spoons as you test my patience
Savoring the few seconds we have together
Tasting this moment
Or so I thought
Yet there you are fidgeting in your chair with a sanguine
    expression
On your fifty-year-old face
Eyebrows scrunched, wrinkles expanding, eyes fixated on the
    tantalizing words in a
Book thinking of another place not here
Moving through various books while I pause and think
Now you are reticent
Where is the vitality that existed yesterday?
When our bodies once twisted like a vine uprooting moments
    of excess
Smashing our broken promises into the fire that is our lust
Turning over the pages of troubled times into the past
Today on this mundane Monday afternoon you beckoned for
    me
As though I was your lackey boy
Yet we are here as the rain caresses the pavement gently
    outside
It's a sun shower with sunlight on the horizon
Almost I could touch you
Like last night as my fingers raced against your articulate,
    analytical, British hands
I believed that I understood you better
Except you feign your nationality
You are not from England but Zimbabwe
This is your theatrical stage production
You're not Othello, Hamlet, or even King Lear
This isn't the Globe Theatre

I listened intently though soaking in your rhetoric
Africa is thousands of miles away from your memory
Of a turbulent time where suffering and death coexisted
You always ignored Africa
I detested your performance at the last lecture
Instead you decided to discuss dead bones, uninhabited
        villages, and foreign times
Where is your passion?
Of boisterous, bountiful, brilliant kisses
Travelling on my arms, legs, thighs, lips, was your sensuous
        tongue
Now you flipped through stacked books on European history
I dreamt of visiting tombs of Pharaohs, reading hieroglyphics,
        and retracing pyramids
Walking by the Nile River was my next destination
Boring Europe was on your first set of plans
Why though?
Does Great Britain provide a sanctuary for your shame?
The cradle bed of colonialism and toxi-racism say anything to
        you
I was perplexed as the fortune cookie arrived
You ignored me as you usually do as I read the message
        silently
Enough of these stacked books!
You cling on to them and not me!
These broad, shiny, dark brown five-hundred-paged turnovers
        incense me!
Carefully you devour the messages within them
The Eurocentric obsession that has enslaved you
A world that is not even your own
Dusty, old relics of pretentious knowledge you crave
Do you actually think you are now more wise?
Revisiting the past will unlock the present into your
        subconscious

Not Knowing You

I feel like a stalker
Lurking in the background
I am the hunter you are prey
Except we are not in the grasslands or the plains of Kenya Africa
Our hunting ground is the suburbs of Toronto
Everyday I see you with your fresh black dreadlock hair
I peak through the creme-coloured blinds wondering if you are
        real
I grab my cock and jerk it thinking of you
I can smell your musty, masculine, cologne, scent
I can taste the black stubble across your hard solid face
I can almost feel you
I can pull off the layers of my clothes

Except not right now
Is this just a dream or a fantasy?
On this breezy Tuesday morning the wind blows delicately on to
        your strong ebony face
Walking your blonde, chiselled, bombshell wife to the car
You hug her as her balloon-sized breasts press against your body
The neighbours cutting their lawns gawk with quiescent disgust
The *for sale* signs are already plastered across the street and down
        the block
This area of town is blue country
Your forbidden love is not accepted here

Your world is complete like winning the lottery
You get to screw everyone all over
Every day is supposed to be like a jackpot
Your two children jump into the shiny green polished station
        wagon with her
Laughing and giggling back at you

The six-year-old girl with long frizzy golden brown curls plays
        with a doll
A boy only five with a large black afro smiles back
You kiss your beloved softly on her ruby red lips
Her almond eyes twinkle back at you
She blows you a kiss
She drives off into the horizon

Not knowing your words are suicide messages
Not knowing you should be penitent
Not knowing that five minutes later I will be seduced on your
        matrimonial bed

Not knowing your fresh chocolate lips will glide over the guy
next door
Not knowing our bodies will be in an inferno of pleasure for
        about an hour

Is it really pleasure though or something more complicated?
Only you know this riddle
The bittersweet taste of your acid-tinged lips
Thinking about your kid's birthday party last week
On that gorgeous Saturday afternoon on the fresh green lawn
I sat in my house watching from a distance
You never acknowledged my existence
Now I am a body a commodity for the moment
Today for the second time we are trapped here in your soiled
        garage

The silence is the answer
Everyone on the block knows of course
Of our afternoon appointments
Except your beloved
She not knowing me
Not knowing you

If

If I tell you now what I knew then
If I allowed you to see what was beneath me
If I refused to look into your solemn, salacious, slivering, eyes
If I let your sensual, seductive, sinister tongue touch my skin
If my river of tears ran like a current of water remembering
        you
If I tried to stop kissing your tender, tingling, thick lips
If I remembered to forget about your wedding day
        photograph
If I still love you
If I don't care about me
If it was meant to be
Let it be

No Answers

We are not thinking
Inside this so called "paradise"
Paid the twenty dollar fee
To finally be me
To not have to dream
About being free
To finally be a man
That some say I can't be
I deserve to be me

In the towering halls
Made of salacious sin
On the outskirts of town
We are free to feel sexy in sweaty cotton towels
Cover over genitals
Tongue moist over hairy balls
Everyone loves black tonight
The weed serenades you
Music is pumping
Bartender is cracking jokes with the loyal followers
The business executives, the garbage men, the judges,
Come here every week

We glide across the cold linoleum floor
While boys glare
From watching the Friday movies
The door is wide open
For any man to be a man
In one room six black and white men groping
The next four blonde, brunette, and Asian guys stroking
Enter the misty dungeon
See the bodybuilder, the baseball, and movie star
Doing their thing in the corner

No one would believe they are here
Their mouths soaked with spit, semen and lust
The drenched skins
Sizzling over
Hard-bodied flesh
That gyrate, that turn, that kiss, that touch
Yes skin burning
Together
In the dark tunnels
We are not realizing

Pleasure is pressure
Explaining the reason for all this
But of course we can't
We grind
We fuck
We are who
We must be because
We answer to
No One

Aladdin Was Slain

Aladdin was a boyfriend of mine
Back when I was eighteen
Back when I believed in love
Now I don't
Love never conquers all
Especially for an old man like me
With a heart so bitter, so cold, so cold,
A soul that's wretched, that's fucking stone

He told me black is beautiful
No black man ever told me that
First time I ever heard that from a nonblack
First second I laid eyes on him I knew . . .
First moment I kissed his dark skin,
Felt his smooth touch
Oh those blissful 1990s
We were young and carefree
Only three months we lasted
But I feel for him for an eternity
He told me though he was running out of time
He kissed me farewell from Pearson
Telling me he will come back
Aladdin has no nation
Clearly he wishes he had a foundation
His brother was blown up in Gaza at age twenty-two
His mother and father don't have a clue
That Aladdin lived a new life in Canada with me
He writes thoughtfully says there is apartheid there
Routine checkpoints, passports, certificates needed
to just do errands!
High unemployment, disease, famine,
Yet Aladdin still feels like a parasite
He says people think he's a murderer up here
Just because he's not from here
I tell him I feel the same way sometimes

Aladdin says if his people found out about us
He would be stabbed in the back in Arabia
Aladdin doesn't want to marry any girl
He says he loves me
How can this be true though Aladdin?

Aladdin wouldn't be free
He's gone
I ask Aladdin what's his choice
He says Canada is better
Being with me
But duty calls
I pray
I pray
I cry
I deny
I sigh
I wait
I wait
I wait
For Aladdin's return
Please Aladdin
Return
To me!

Pedro

Oh my love
The pain of dreams
Of recollection
Your feverish kisses, your olive skin
Still enrapture me
Your intelligence, your are like a good luck charm
You know everything
I know, I know
Even though twenty-five years separated us
You loved me better than a young man could
You showed me what reciprocity means
Still nightmares rape me in the night
Wondering where we went wrong
Wandering to and from anguish and loneliness
Sauntering, pacing, walking alone
The line of balance
Rumbling, tossing, turning,
Crashing down is the agony of our love
Rising above the surface of the lies
Visiting you was tragic
It shattered all the mythology of my mind
Opening me up to humanity
I invaded your privacy
You never wanted me to see
The real you

Yes, it was brief
Your manhood had the power to change the world
Your strength captured me
You held me, loved me better than any man
You had the machismo and the courage

This
Travelling together
Oh I wish
We could splash in the turquoise sea
the magic of the Azores and dance and sing
You promised me
We could see the Iberian Peninsula
Why did I trust you?
Oh I wonder
How we could visit Porto or Lisbon
We could dance and you could sing to me
Tell me why? why? why?
Pedro you wore a mask
A mirage in another universe
Battling the pain within yourself
You pushed me over the mountain of veracity
I tumbled into the inconsolable world of reality
Pedro, Pedro, Pedro
Speak to me now
We cannot turn back time no more
Tell me, show me, feel me,
I still believe
I still I still
I still
Think
of
You

It

When you heard it in a sentence
The sword stabbed the back
An atomic bomb exploded inside like Hiroshima
I dropped it as it shattered dreams into ten million fragments
The obituary is ready
Ambition is a fading, foggy, dream
Words strike the essence of memory
It kills faster than a bullet
Life is a ripped open heart

The Good Son

My father didn't say it but I am not the good son
I am not macho, strong, and athletic like my older omnipotent
        brother
He is self-absorbed, brash, arrogant, while I continue to fade
        into the background
He has controlled me mentally for the past two decades since
        birth
Where were you when he mistreated me?
You only watched in the distance not wanting to interfere
When my face was swollen and bloody did you not notice?
Was I not clear that I was terrified when I called the police back
        in 1994?
Boys will be boys you say
I guess all the boys get degraded and emotionally destroyed
        just like me
My bedroom was my refuge from the strange feelings I had
        been having
I am numb and indifferent to everyone

On the walls there are photographs of happier days
Now I wish I didn't have the bloody lip and I was happy

Reality

Reality says black is bad
Truth is I always knew that
Even though my momma and papa told me otherwise
Even though I read black history
The text book definition of black is
Reality
I flicked on the tube last night
I never knew I am destined to become a drug dealer
I saw my five baby mothers complaining about me on television
The news anchors called one of my brothers a menace to society
I looked at his gold teeth, corn rolls, and ebony sweet velvet skin
I saw his black face plastered across the screen
He is filthy, grotesque, and evil
I am told this is my reality
That I too will end up in the clink
Or six feet deep
Funny, I never hear the same thing said about the
White boys
The pale men that beat murder and rape
They are pop stars like Charles Manson and Paul Bernardo
They are serenaded
While my brothers are
Scorned
Why?
This is reality

The Trail of Blood Stops Here

Are black men the losers of the world?
If we don't follow that "silent" rule?
Guess he can't be gay?
He can't love another black man
He can't kiss another brother
Touch his smooth thick chocolate lips
His warm ebony touch
His sensual healing tongue
Hold his hands when he
Cries in the dark
Work with him
Embrace him
Love him
Treat him with respect
With some dignity
He can't be the artist unless he's a rap artist
He should be the academic writer
But why should he?
He could be the school teacher
Might be a father who works for minimum wage
A school principal
Should I shoot a hoop into a basket?
Hit a baseball?
Wear sparkling jewelry?
Rhyme about sex?
Run track and field?
Wear some gold teeth?
Walk down the street growling
Speak incoherently like a drunk?
Should I rape your sister, daughter, mother, or grandmother?
Will I be down?
Will I be cool?
Will I be a "real brother" if I rob that bank?

If I don't do well in life?
Will I be "representing" if I just watch you beat the
Shit out of your girlfriend or baby mama
Will I be "a man" if I don't take care of my family?
Shoot a police officer?
Then I will be "really black"
Rob a bank?
Be a gangster?
Death stood in front of me
All the way from Jamaica
Your message was clear

We Struggle

From the shores of West Africa to the new world we struggle
The shadows of the whipping, raping, and murdering still
    linger
The fortunate few that survived the ocean's crossing endured
    the madness
Young mothers kill their babies to protect them from impurity
Off the coast of New York City there was vindictiveness
A dark man reached for his wallet and paid the price
He died forty-one times since America has no remorse, justice,
    or truth
From the bones of the dead to the blood in my veins we still
    struggle
Institutionalized slavery still exists except now it's written
    down into books
You have to be white for the pendulum to shift in your favour
We say success is the best revenge this too is a lie
We still struggle

Skin Deep

"What is beauty" I asked myself
Some people say it's only skin deep
I say I am dark and lovely
My skin is black as coal and warm like fire
The richness of my skin protects me from the sun
I don't thicken my lips to fit in
Nor do I thin my nose or bleach myself
My hair is nappy, nappy, and coarse
I am dark and lovely so let it be

When I Breathe

When I breathe
I take all of the world in
The disease, the plague
The frustration and the sin
I exhale
Watching the clouds above in the turbulent sky
Washing away
The residue within
I no longer have to wonder why the pain will dim
When I breathe I know
That I no longer have to begin

Only White Girls

They say only white girls do this
Yet here I am on
My hands and knees
In front of the ceramic toilet
My inhibitions betrayed me
Imperfectly
Time and time again
Like an alcoholic during a drunken binge
I keep on asking for more
Nothing is ever certain these days
That lasts for an eternity
As I devour everything in sight
Never waiting for a moment, one moment to say
Enough
It's too late for enough
Enough doesn't resist temptation
It cannot hold back the inevitable
This drug, this attraction, this hunger, that I crave is elusive
It's like bad sex
Going through the rudimentary motions
Of more consequences yet no feeling
And no peace
A detour of false promises unfulfilled
The strife is psychological they say
A cathartic neurosis that acts as a catalyst
It's a toxic stew of chocolate cake, ice cream, and wine
As failures are expunged
From within as it swirls, moving swiftly through
Misty, murky, misrepresented, judgments escaped
It's a blotched mess of lost dreams, hopes, and fears that is
        a brilliant dark brown
The routine is continued night after night
End result is still the same

Bloodshot eyes engorged with discontent continued this
       façade
Fingers tingle as the brown glob covers sweaty hands
Hair dishevelled due to days of darkness
Legs were too loose like jelly
I flung myself to the tiled floor
In front of the grimy green mat
Seconds felt like hours
Again the process is started
This is a circus
A comedy of errors that continues
Pain squeezes through the esophagus
It scorches like an explosion
The red, rueful, restless, rawness of the stress compresses me
Sizzling poison through burning lips
The equilibrium will never be in place
As few more slurps of cola later I pass out
Into a world where reflections don't matter
It's a false prayer
Of rambling thoughts, combined with sentences that can't
       change this prophecy
It's a divine intervention
Now fate strikes down
She moves quickly her answer is an omen in disguise
Refuses to cut the string that is life
Perhaps contemplating a second wind, a second opportunity
A foolish gesture that wavers
This frantic, frenetic, frivolous, routine
Skins, faces, legs, and arms are a resume
A blueprint that is scrutinized, categorized, and stigmatized,
Why can't I have it all?
This is bittersweet
Yet I diagnose this condition as a lack of strength

She Is Positive

Who is positive?
She is positive
How?
By her husband in Africa
Because?
The African tale is virgins are pure they aren't
Positive
Teen-aged girls are firm with large breasts, tight
        bodies, tight between their legs
What does positive mean?
Death death death death death death
Separate invisible barriers are torture
Worse than Jim Crow laws
Harsher than a lynching
She would rather slit her child's throat
She would rather be shot with a bullet
Than live through the pain in agony
Positive + Black = silence
She is now a leper
The grandmothers raise the orphans alone
In remote villages
There is treatment in the north but
Not for dark-skinned folks
Not for her
In Cape Town, The Congo, Botswana, Lesotho,
She dies silently, tragically,
Because the world doesn't care that she is
Positive

Days

During days of boredom
As the raging tsunami of apathy decreases
I read tasting the succulent saccharine words in a book
Devouring the nourishment of sentences and paragraphs
I can hike up steep mountains and kiss the sun
I will travel to the depths of the earth and across continents
I wonder as I wander
While the midnight sun shines giving me freedom to believe
That I am real

Before You Commit Suicide

Don't close the blinds of truth
You can't eclipse the weighty anchor of brutality!
Stop being so pusillanimous!
When you envision the inevitable
Please think of me
Don't be esoteric!
Embrace the pain wrap it around you
Squeeze this despair
prick the memory like a needle
Sew the threads of wondering
Open the fresh wound that's the stench of misery
Failures are broken unrequited desires and promises
Recall the dysfunction are like smashed lost artifacts
Yes they are ruins trapped in the attic of the mind
Run down broad boxes that are molding
Why? Why? Why?
Cruel destiny
How many times can one fall down?
Hatred is a vaccine
Is there ever a way up?
Self doubt was never a cure
No one knows no one cares
Move beyond this like turning a page
Don't erase this event

This Fatal Kiss

The mellifluous sounds of his tongue glides across my neck,
I'm slightly nervous
Pulling at my black turtleneck sleeve
Yet the bravado as the blue velvet jazz music illuminates
        the smoky crowded bar
The paucity of our love is mendacious yet I am in an alluring
        trance as my beloved's
warm chestnut brown eyes twirl like an emaciated ballet
        dancer
He's bold he places his enigmatic black hand onto mine
I laugh as he ingratiates me with another pitcher of frothy
        beer
Placing his salacious, caramel lips onto mine
He tastes secretive, seductive, sensual, like bitter, black, dark,
        melting chocolate
Tonight he is loquacious as his perfidious words drip into my
        bruised heart like acid
My fingers though press against his mahogany sweater acrosss
        his bulging biceps
On the horizon his sparking ring blinds me
He kisses me again as an electrical surge penetrates and
        numbs me
I pull away seeing mirages regretting this fatal kiss